Selfless or Selfish

CHALLENGE
BIBLE STUDY GUIDES

Old Testament Women by Sara Buswell
   Believers or Beguilers
   Courageous Overcomers
   Vain or Visionary
   Selfless or Selfish

When God Calls by Sara Buswell
   Responding to God's Call
   Submitting to God's Call

The Life of David by Mary Nelle Schaap
   Seeing God in the Life of Young David
   Seeing God in the Life of David the King

Portraits of Jesus from the Gospel Writers by Mary Nelle Schaap
   Portraits of Jesus from Matthew and Mark
   Portraits of Jesus from Luke and John

Studies in Old Testament Poetry by Kathleen Buswell Nielson
   This God We Worship
   Resting Secure

Selfless or Selfish

Old Testament Women

Sara Buswell

BAKER BOOK HOUSE
Grand Rapids, Michigan 49516

Contents

Introduction

This book is an invitation to meet women of the Old Testament, and to apply principles of God's character and design seen in them to your own personality and circumstances. The text and study questions are intended to facilitate your acquaintance with these women who, after all, are not very different from yourself. To be a woman today, pleasing to God and transformed to the image of his likeness, is a high calling, a real challenge. But God has not left us without models to warn and to welcome us along the way.

The relevance of each Bible character to the needs of each reader will be different. You may not agree with the applications suggested by other members of your group or in the printed text of this book. That is not important. What matters is that you grow closer to God as you realize that his Word is living and active, and that he desires to make himself known to you personally. As you become acquainted with these women, your relationship with the Lord will deepen as well.

There is always more to discover in God's living Word, even within a narrow range of study. Remember the guidelines and the purpose of your search as we have begun it together. Don't water down the Scriptures or weaken the punch of its message. Let each woman speak from within her own context. With prayer and imagination, put yourself in her situation, and invite God to reveal and apply his relevant principles to your life through her story. Don't indulge in fantasy. Fake jewels have no value, however attractive they may be. The Bible is true, its characters real historical people just as we are. What a privilege we have to know our God, and ourselves, through its study and application. The challenge continues. I pray you will enjoy it and share it as you grow.

Study Plan

1. Read the questions at the beginning of each lesson.

2. Read the Scripture passage(s) listed and be aware of the questions as you read. Allow time to think about words or phrases or incidents that are especially meaningful to you. Underline them in your Bible.

3. Formulate initial answer(s) to questions.

4. If possible, discuss answers with a friend or group.

5. Read the lesson commentary.

6. Revise answers, if necessary.

7. Apply your answers to your life as God directs.

1

Zipporah

Primary Scripture Reading	Supplementary Reference
Exodus 3, 4, and 18	2 Corinthians 6:14

Questions for Study and Discussion

1. Who was Zipporah? Whom did she marry? Why?

   Wife of Moses —

   Do you think she was well suited to be the wife of such a man? Why or why not?

   — had deep spiritual understanding
   — supportive

2. Read the passage about the circumcision of Moses' son (Exod. 4) in as many different translations as you can. Why was it necessary?

   Genesis 17 - Ex 14 — It was God's appointed sign of the covenant — to signify Moses commitment to God

   What attitude do you think lay behind Zipporah's words and actions in that scene? Was she being obedient or defiant? Of whom?

   Obedient to God.

3. Why didn't Zipporah participate in the exodus from Egypt with Moses? Did someone send her back to Midian, or did she refuse to go on with her husband?

11

4. Think about some of your personal and professional relationships. How could you convince your partner to carry out God's will without your destroying the partnership?

What warnings do you draw from Zipporah's example concerning God's standard of "equal yoking" (see 2 Cor. 6:14)?

Moses married an alien woman!

5. Perhaps Zipporah's behavior could be explained in terms of her lack of trust in Moses or in God. Was it fair for her to be excluded from the exodus for this reason, rather than to be given the opportunity to develop her faith?

What do you learn about God's requirement of faith from this story? Are you going forward or backward in your spiritual life?

6. How do you interpret the reunion of Moses with his wife, children, and father-in-law after the exodus (Exod. 18)? Did any members of Zipporah's family stay with Moses during the years of wandering in the desert? Why, or why not?

*Z*ipporah is mentioned in three separate chapters of Exodus. Moses married her, returned to Egypt without her, and had a brief reunion with her after he successfully led the Israelites to freedom. The adage "Behind every great man is a great woman" can be applied literally to Zipporah—Moses left her *far* behind! How did she miss out on becoming a full partner in her husband's great mission, and what can we learn from her example?

Family Background

First, we need to consider Moses himself. When he was forty years old he killed an Egyptian guard who was beating a Hebrew slave, and fled the country. It was his choice to marry Zipporah and work as a shepherd for her father Jethro (or Reuel) for forty years before God called him back to Egypt (see Acts 7:29–34 as well as Exod. 1–3 for the context). But Moses' idea was not to abandon his wife in Midian just so he could go after fame and fortune in his homeland. In fact, God had quite a hard time convincing Moses to go, and had to promise him three signs in addition to the oratorical support of his brother Aaron before he agreed. Even so, Moses begged, "O Lord, please send someone else to do it" (Exod. 4:13).

Moses' humility was reflected throughout his period of leadership. He was acutely aware of his own verbal deficiencies. "O LORD, I have never been eloquent, neither in the past nor since you have spoken to your servant. I am slow of speech and tongue" (Exod. 4:10). He depended on Aaron's help in speaking to the Egyptian rulers as well as to his own people. His sister Miriam also shared some of the responsibilities of leadership with him. In addition, he welcomed a suggestion from his father-in-law to appoint captains and judges to lighten his burden. Numbers 12:3 states, "Now Moses was a very humble man, more humble than anyone else on the face of the earth." All this evidence demonstrates the fact that Moses needed and appreciated the support of his family. God's summons to Moses to return to Egypt in no way provided him with an ego trip or a deliberate attempt to reject the wife and lifestyle he had enjoyed in Midian. Moses would not have chosen to set aside Zipporah had she not shown herself to be ineligible to join with him in fulfilling God's appointed task.

What do we actually know about Zipporah? Technically, she was not an Israelite, nor did she experience bondage with them in Egypt. Her father was Jethro, a priest of the Midianites, who were descended from the fourth son of Abraham by Keturah (q.v.). The Midianites were closely connected with the Ishmaelites in Arabia (see Gen. 37). Because of this association we might say that strong regional, if not racial or religious, ties prevailed to keep Zipporah at home, or possibly prevented her from generating much sympathy for the plight of the Israelites in Egypt. We could then point to her example as evidence of the incompatibility that is bound to emerge in a marriage of a believer with an unbeliever (see 2 Cor. 6:14).

Family background is really too simplistic an explanation of Zipporah's disqualification, however. With the same history, both her father and her brother became much more enthusiastically and extensively involved with Moses and the Israelites. After the exodus, Jethro's reunion with his son-in-law was ebullient.

> Now Jethro, the priest of Midian and father-in-law of Moses, heard of everything God had done for Moses and for his people Israel, and how the LORD had brought Israel out of Egypt. . . . Jethro was delighted to hear about all the good things the LORD had done for Israel in rescuing them from the hand of the Egyptians. He said, "Praise be to the LORD, who rescued you from the hand of the Egyptians and of Pharaoh, and who rescued the people from the hand of the Egyptians. Now I know that the LORD is greater than all other gods, for he did this to those who had treated Israel arrogantly" (Exod. 18:1, 9–11).

They sacrificed and ate together in the presence of God with all the elders of Israel.

In the midst of this scene of celebration, Zipporah is mentioned only in passing, and somewhat coolly.

> After Moses had sent away his wife Zipporah, his father-in-law Jethro received her and her two sons. . . . Jethro, Moses' father-in-law, together with Moses' sons and wife, came to him in the desert where he was camped near the mountain of God. Jethro had sent word to him, "I, your father-in-law Jethro, am coming to you with your wife and her two sons." So Moses went out to meet his father-in-law and bowed down and kissed him. . . . Moses told his father-in-law about everything the LORD had done to Pharaoh and the Egyptians for Israel's sake and about all the hardships they had met along the way and how the LORD had saved them (Exod. 18:2–8).

It seems that Zipporah was present but not a full participant in the welcoming party. The father-in-law's relationship with Moses was both warmer and deeper.

Similarly, Jethro's son Hobab (presumably Zipporah's brother and therefore Moses' brother-in-law) apparently continued his association with the Israelites for an even longer period. In Numbers 10:29–33, Moses begged him to remain as their guide, promising to share with him "whatever good things the LORD gives us." Although Hobab's initial response was, "No, I will not go. I am going back to my own land and my own people" (Num. 10:30), he apparently traveled with them for some time. Later, Hobab's descendants, the Kenites, are remembered for their kindness to Israel (Judg. 4:9–24 and 1 Sam. 15:6). Family ties cannot be blamed for Zipporah's detachment from her husband's assigned purpose.

Holding Back

Ethnic identity is never God's primary criterion for inclusion among his chosen people; rather, personal faith was and is the sole standard. Zipporah did not share with Moses the personal faith in God necessary to support his unique ministry or even to survive the arduous journey and trials which lay ahead for him.

Jesus warned, "No man can serve two masters. Either he will hate the one and love the other, or he will be devoted to the one and despise the other" (Matt. 6:24). He offers us a choice between God and Mammon. In Moses' case, Zipporah was functioning in the role of Mammon, the pull of the world and its desires. Moses (or any husband) could not sustain for long the tension between the leading forward of God and the pulling back of his wife. It seems that she was not able to release her husband *wholeheartedly* to the Lord, a problem that is both familiar and challenging for us today. Moses had to make the difficult decision to send her back to Jethro in order to fulfill God's greater purpose for his own life and for his people.

How can I infer that Zipporah would have interfered with Moses' ministry? Because she did so, in an important incident recorded in a confusing passage in Exodus 4. Let us consider several translations of verses 24–26, in order better to understand the event and its implications.

> And it came to pass by the way in the inn, that the LORD met him [Moses] and sought to kill him. Then Zipporah took a sharp stone, and cut off the foreskin of her son, and cast it at his feet, and said, Surely a bloody husband . . . thou art, because of the circumcision (King James Version).

> At a lodging place on the way the LORD met him and sought to kill him. Then Zipporah took a flint and cut off her son's foreskin, and touched Moses' feet with it and said, "Surely you are a bridegroom of blood," . . . because of the circumcision (Revised Standard Version).

> At an inn on the way the LORD met him and was at the point of taking his life; but Zipporah took a flint knife, cir-

cumcised her son and threw the foreskin at his feet with the words, "You are indeed a blood bridegroom to me." Then he let him alone when she said, because of the circumcision, "You are my bridegroom in blood" (Modern Language).

As Moses and his family were traveling along and had stopped for the night, Jehovah appeared to Moses and threatened to kill him. Then Zipporah his wife took a flint knife and cut off the foreskin of her young son's penis, and threw it against Moses' feet, remarking disgustedly, "What a blood-smeared husband you've turned out to be!" Then God let him alone (Living Bible).

At a lodging place on the way, the LORD met Moses and was about to kill him. But Zipporah took a flint knife, cut off her son's foreskin and touched Moses' feet with it. "Surely you are a bridegroom of blood to me," she said. So the LORD let him alone. (At that time she said "bridegroom of blood," referring to circumcision) (New International Version).

The problem here is not to choose our favorite version but the most accurate. Rather than becoming more confused, I hope we can have greater respect and appreciation for the difficult task of Bible translation through this exercise. This passage is important to our understanding of Moses, Zipporah, and God himself.

Several questions may be raised. Why would God call Moses to return to Egypt and then try to kill him on the way? How did Zipporah know that circumcising their son Gershom would gain Moses' release from the Lord? Was she right in performing the rite? What attitudes toward Moses and toward God were reflected in her actions? The various texts offer us several possible interpretations with only partial information. Still, several observations can be made about this incident that may provide useful applications to various situations in our lives.

Everything I know about God's character tells me that he was not trying to kill Moses, but only wanted to get his attention about a serious matter that needed to be dealt with before he got all the way to Egypt. God had commanded circumcision of all Hebrew males as a sign of his covenant with Abraham (see Gen. 17:9–14). It was to be performed on the eighth day of life, or upon conversion. Moses had failed to obey this commandment in regard to his sons prior to his trip, but it was an act that was essential not only for his own training but also for the Egyptians' understanding of the importance of the covenant, and for the credibility of Moses as a leader in the eyes of the Israelites.

Zipporah seems to have saved Moses' life by performing the circumcision of Gershom just in time. Why was she not appreciated for her quick-thinking rescue? For one thing, circumcision was a male-only activity. Women were excluded from participation at every level—as patient, witness, or surgeon. But it was her attitude rather than her act that caused Zipporah to be sent back to Jethro with her sons. There was a touch of bitterness and reproach as she threw the bloody foreskin at Moses' feet with an air of "Now look what I had to do to save your neck!" Again we see a wife who obeyed God in her deed but not in her heart, which was, and is, not enough for the Lord.

Zipporah had started out on the journey to Egypt with Moses. After the incident at the inn she turned around and went back to her father's house. Exodus 18:2 informs us, "After Moses had sent away his wife Zipporah, his father-in-law Jethro received her and her two sons." It is not clear from the passage in Exodus 4 whether God sent her home, whether Moses refused to let her continue with him, or whether she herself changed her mind about the journey. There is no indication that Zipporah objected to the decision or pleaded for another chance to remain at his side.

The crisis must have revealed to each of them the personal cost of obedience to God. Moses chose to obey. Zipporah did not take that step of faith with him, even though she had acted quickly to save his life. Her outburst expressed her strong, if subconscious, desire not to follow where God and her husband were leading. Perhaps she was even thinking to herself, "For richer, for poorer, but not for this!" as she drew the line that cut off their relationship.

Try to evaluate honestly before God your relationship with the members of your family. Are there limits to how far *you* are willing to go to help your spouse, children, or friends respond to God's direction? Do you offer your wholehearted support, or do you sometimes pull against their commitment to serve God first—an effort to keep at least a corner of the attention on yourself? Is your own commitment wholeheartedly focused on God, or are you too easily distracted by the impression you are trying to make on others? Be careful that you do not put your loved ones in the position of having to choose between satisfying you and serving God.

Zipporah failed to go to Egypt with her husband, but she did have another opportunity to join him after his return, as we have seen in Exodus 18:5–6. It is difficult to determine whether she went back to Midian with Jethro or continued through the wilderness with the Israelites. The Bible does not mention her again. Exodus 18:27 states, "Then Moses sent his father-in-law on his way, and he returned to his own country," without specifying whether Zipporah stayed with her husband or went with her father. My guess is that she parted from Moses a second time. Had she remained, more should have been recorded of her, including some record of her death, if not other incidents. In particular, it would seem that the story of the confrontation of Aaron and Miriam over Moses' Cushite wife (Num. 12:1) would have contained some mention of Zipporah had she still been part of the family at that point. Throughout the account of her life Moses just doesn't seem to pay her much attention either at the time of their reunion or afterward.

Zipporah's rejection, both *of* and *by* Moses, was largely of her own making. Even though I wish that the account were more complete so that I could know for certain what became of her, I do not suppose, from reading the passages we do have, that Zipporah was any more capable of joining her husband on the journey to the Promised Land than of traveling to Egypt to take part in the exodus. Lacking a personal relationship of total trust with God, she was not able to look or move toward a new horizon in either direction. Thus, she was set aside from service. Where is God trying to move you? Are you willing to go, or will you be left behind or left out when others step forward in obedience?

2

Hagar

Primary Scripture Reading

Genesis 16:1–18; 18:15; 21

Supplementary References

James 4:2–8
Isaiah 43:1–3
Hebrews 12:2–3
1 Peter 5:6–7

Questions for Study and Discussion

1. What was Hagar's native land? What do you know about the range of duties and privileges she might have expected for herself in Abram's household?

2. What was she told to do for her master? Did she have any choice in the matter?

   Was this command out of the ordinary according to Hagar's culture and position? Did her status change as a result?

3. In which verse do you find a different attitude in Hagar than at first? Why did her feelings change? What happened as a direct result?

Did Hagar have any control over these circumstances?

Have you chosen to despise someone? What consequences ensued? If you feel you have suffered rejection, is there some action or an attitude on your part that contributed to that rejection? Could it have been avoided?

4. Compare God's two meetings with Hagar that are described in Genesis 16 and 21. What did he tell her to do? What was his purpose?

Do you detect any spiritual development in Hagar in the second encounter as compared with the first?

5. Consider Ishmael's behavior and its consequences in Genesis 21:9. Whose attitude was he reflecting?

In what ways have you noticed your feelings rubbing off on other people? Give some better ways of resolving your feelings.

6. What evidences of pride do you detect in Hagar's story? How is this sin connected with her rejection from Abraham's household?

What significance do you find in the fact that Hagar found a wife in Egypt for Ishmael? Are there manifestations of pride in your life?

7. Compare the attitude expressed by Hagar's actions with the New Testament verses listed above, which present God's example and expectation of service. What lessons in humility do you need to apply to your life at home or at work today?

*B*eing an Egyptian maidservant, Hagar had almost no part in the decisions concerning her household duties or personal life that her master and mistress, Abram and Sarai, made. In the culture of that time and place it was not unusual for a man to have sexual relations with any and all of the women in his household; multiple wives, concubines, or whole harems of slaves or captives are frequently mentioned in the Bible. This practice, though common, was never endorsed by God, however. Numerous passages indicate his high standard of monogamy (Gen. 2:24; Deut. 17:16–17; 1 Tim. 3:12).

The essential purpose of marriage, in the minds of Abram's contemporaries, was for a man to produce legitimate children, preferably male offspring, to inherit and defend his name and possessions after him. The selection of one slave girl over another to accomplish this purpose—in case of a wife's failure in this requirement—might have been made in recognition of her beauty or loyalty, but it would not have constituted a major or unreasonable deviation from accepted behavior. It was quite common for a barren wife to adopt her slave's children as her own, as Sarai proposed (later Rachel and Leah did the same; see Gen. 30). For Hagar to serve the function of preserving the family line of Abram could have been just one of a number of household duties she was expected to perform. It was only the fact that Sarai and Abram failed to grasp the full miracle of God's promise to them, and instead resorted to methods of their own, that made their conduct wrong. Hagar's sin was not in conceiving and bearing a child to Abram, but in her arrogant behavior that followed both acts. Perhaps she had no voice concerning what was done to her, but she *did* have a choice regarding her response. Hagar chose to despise, to keep distant, and to disseminate hostility to the next generation.

Choice to Despise

In Genesis 15, God promised Abram offspring as numerous as the stars of the heavens. A son would come from his own body, and his descendants would inherit the land of Canaan.

> Now Sarai, Abram's wife, had borne him no children. But she had an Egyptian maidservant named Hagar; so she said to Abram, "The LORD has kept me from having children. Go, sleep with my maidservant; perhaps I can build a family through her." Abram agreed to what Sarai said. So after Abram had been living in Canaan ten years, Sarai his wife took her Egyptian maidservant Hagar and gave her to her husband to be his wife. He slept with Hagar, and she conceived (Gen. 16:1–4).

Throughout this entire transaction Hagar was viewed by Sarai and Abram merely as a tool to gain a specific objective, a child. After ten years of childlessness in Canaan, Sarai finally suggested a new approach, and Abram carried it out. Apparently the Lord was not consulted, and neither was Hagar.

We might be inclined to sympathize with Hagar's plight if this scene of sexual exploitation were all that we knew about her. She loses our respect at once, however, when we read of the marked change in her attitude recorded afterwards in Genesis 16:4: "When she knew she was pregnant, she began to despise her mistress." Although she had not engineered her circumstances at the outset, she *was* responsible for making the situation intolerable for the entire household by her sudden switch from apparent compliance to open arrogance.

We know, because the whole story has been recorded and retold for centuries, that God had intended from the beginning to bless Abram through Sarai's own child by his miraculous "quickening" (KJV) of their bodies, and that Ishmael, Hagar's son, was never meant to be the child of promise (see Gen. 17:18–22; 21:12; also Gal. 4:22–31). Their alternate plan to use Hagar was indicative of their own undeveloped faith up to that time.

Nevertheless, Hagar had an active role in choosing to despise her mistress, and thereby bringing on herself an increase in suffering. Had she sought to overcome her emotions, she would probably not have incurred Sarai's "hardness" (KJV), which caused her first to flee to the wilderness (Gen. 16:5–6) and later to be sent forth with Ishmael (Gen. 21:9–14). Is there a person whom you have chosen to despise because of the way he or she has treated you? In what ways has your response made the situation better or worse for yourself and for others?

Choice to Keep Distant

Once we realize that Hagar was her own catalyst, making her difficult situation worse, we can move on to consider whether she learned anything from the experiences of God meeting her twice in the wilderness. Two distinct passages record Hagar's encounters with God, which may be placed in a chart for comparison.

	Genesis 16:6–16	Genesis 21:14–22
Why Hagar left:	Sarai mistreated her.	Abraham sent her out with Ishmael, bread and water.
Where she went:	Near a spring in the desert, beside the road to Shur	In the desert of Beersheba
How she felt:	Probable fear, self-pity	Expected the death of Ishmael, wept
What the angel of the LORD said:	"Hagar, servant of Sarai, where have you come from, and where are you going?" "Go back to your mistress and submit to her. I will so increase your descendants that they will be too numerous to count. You are now with child and you will have a son. You shall name him Ishmael, for the Lord has heard of your misery. He will be a wild donkey of a man; his hand will be against everyone and everyone's hand against him, and he will live in hostility toward all his brothers."	"What is the matter, Hagar? Do not be afraid; God has heard the boy crying as he lies there. Lift the boy up and take him by the hand, for I will make him into a great nation."
What God did:		Opened Hagar's eyes and she saw a well of water. God was with the boy as he grew up.
Outcome:	Hagar gave a name to the Lord and to the well *Lahai Roi,* "the Living One who sees me."	Hagar got water for Ishmael. He grew up, lived in the desert, and became an archer. While he was living in the Desert of Paran, his mother got a wife for him from Egypt.

There is a lot we don't know about Hagar before, between, and after these encounters with the angel of the Lord. We cannot really judge her overall level of spiritual commitment. But in looking at the chart above, there does not seem to be any marked development in her relationship with God from the first of these experiences to the second, a separation of approximately fifteen years.

True, Hagar had not been called to a personal ministry by God. Being a foreigner, she should be given credit, at the least, for recognizing God's presence and following his direct commands—first to return to Sarai and name the child Ishmael, and later to get up and get water for her son. She responded honestly enough to God's inquiries and commands. But she did not grow to any deeper understanding of his person or plans, as Abraham and Sarai did. The last we are told of Hagar is that she provided Ishmael with a wife from Egypt, her own place of origin. We would have expected the same had she never interacted at all with her master and mistress or their God.

Are you content to have a static relationship with God from year to year? In what ways has your awareness of his love deepened in the last five, fifteen, or even thirty years, so that you depend more joyfully, and less nervously, on his concern and care? Do you worship him, but expect him to keep his distance and not interfere with your self-determined personality and plans, and not instruct you to deal with the difficult people and circumstances in your life?

Hagar's experiences help me to realize that not only does God want to meet me wherever I am, but also that he wants me to yield and grow closer to him as he leads me each step and each year of my life. He will not force his will on me, just as he did not compel Hagar. But the choice is mine to open the door to receive him when he knocks (see Rev. 3:20).

God was knocking at the door of Hagar's heart when the angel spoke to her on those two occasions we have studied, but she never really admitted him into her life. How can we know this? Although she surely thought and said more than is attributed to her in the biblical narrative, it is interesting to look for an answer in the comments that are included. She is quoted twice in Genesis 16. In verse 8 she responded to God's question with the words, "I'm running away from my mistress Sarai." In verse 13 she gave God a special name and said, "I have now seen the One who sees me." And just before the angel met with her again in Genesis 21, Hagar thought to herself, "I cannot watch the boy die" (Gen. 21:16).

Each of these statements begins with the subject *I*, referring to Hagar. They are simple declarative statements of fact. Hagar never seemed to express her own needs or to ask for God's help in any way, even though her anguish must have been profound on both occasions. Why did she not call on the Lord to provide comfort and care for herself and her son?

We would do well to ask ourselves the same question when we experience periods of either simple discouragement or real rejection. There is no doubt that God's resources to help us are boundless; yet he always desires that we first come to him acknowledging our utter helplessness and humbly seeking his forgiveness, comfort, guidance, strength, and provision (Matt. 11:28–30; James 4:8). Then he is pleased to fill our cups to overflowing (Ps. 23), to do whatever we ask in his name. James confirmed this sequence when he observed, "You do not have because you do not ask God" (James 4:2). Instead of asking and receiving, Hagar chose to keep her distance.

Choice to Disseminate Hostility

We have seen that Hagar chose to despise her mistress and to keep aloof from the personal, powerful God who had twice revealed himself to her. Both choices have important lessons for us today. What else can we learn from this rejected woman?

On the feast day that celebrated Isaac's weaning, Sarah observed Hagar's son "mocking" (Gen. 21:9). Although not all translations of the Bible agree on this word, it is clear that Ishmael did something to rekindle the antagonism that apparently had been smoldering beneath the surface for many years. Whatever it was that he did, his behavior so offended Sarah that she insisted Abraham send him and his mother away once and for all. "Get rid of that slave woman and her son, for that slave woman's son will never share in the inheritance with my son Isaac" (Gen. 21:10).

It would be difficult to imagine any other source of Ishmael's attitude of superiority than his own mother. Although she had managed not to anger Sarah overtly during those intervening years (at least, no further confrontations are recorded in Scripture), it appears that Hagar could not resist sharing her private opinions with Ishmael, who readily adopted her attitudes. She had submitted outwardly, but not inwardly, and thus had transmitted her inner poison to her son.

This pattern reminds me of the story of a small boy whose father attempted to punish him by making him sit in a corner. The boy defiantly insisted on standing, and his father repeatedly shoved him into the chair. After several rounds, the child finally remained in his seat, but was heard to mutter, "I'm sitting on the outside, Pa, but inside I'm still standing."

Here we find another challenge for our lives as we consider Hagar's example. In what ways are you still "standing on the inside" against the authority of God, so that your bad moods and negative attitudes are never healed but continue to fester and poison your life and the lives of others? Instead, will you now choose to pour out your feelings of hurt and rejection to God, who not only sees you but knows your very heart? He can soothe and heal only if you allow him to work his will in your spirit as well as in your difficult situation. Yield yourself fully to him, and claim the full measure of comfort offered in Isaiah 43:1–3:

> Fear not, for I have redeemed you; I have called you by name; you are mine. When you pass through the waters, I will be with you; and when you pass through the rivers, they will not sweep over you. When you walk through the fire, you will not be burned; the flames will not set you ablaze. For I am the LORD, your God, the Holy One of Israel, your Savior.

One last thought. Hagar was a servant, yet she did not have a servant's heart. Christ, in washing the disciples' feet, showed them and us his new standard of humility and service (John 13:1–17). When we feel rejected or depressed, and most of us do from time to time, what a privilege it is to contemplate his perfect example of suffering and submission on our behalf.

> Let us fix our eyes on Jesus, the author and perfecter of our faith, who for the joy set before him endured the cross, scorning its shame, and sat down at the right hand of the throne of God. Consider him who endured such opposition from sinful men, so that you will not grow weary and lose heart (Heb. 12:2–3).

Our suffering, whether due to our own sin or to circumstances over which we have no control, pales in comparison with what Christ endured for us. No matter how many years we must wait in hardship, we can be confident of his continued presence with us, and our eternal presence with him. "Humble yourselves, therefore, under God's mighty hand, that he may lift you up in due time. Cast all your anxiety on him because he cares for you" (1 Peter 5:6–7).

3

Job's Wife

Primary Scripture Reading

Job 1–2 and 42

Supplementary Reference

Matthew 16:23

Questions for Study and Discussion

1. Describe Job's family and property, using the first five verses of Job 1. List some of his blessings.

   What did he do regularly in behalf of his children? What did this practice show about Job's relationship with God?

2. What arrangement did the Lord make with Satan concerning Job? Did Job deserve to be treated this way?

   Why did God allow this test of his servant?

   What limitation did God place on Satan's power to afflict Job?

3. List the sequence of catastrophes that befell Job, using Job 1:13–2:8.

Why was Job's wife not struck down with the rest of the family? Was it in Satan's interest to let her live?

4. What was the advice Job's wife gave to her husband in 2:9? Can you explain his response to her and the comment he made in 2:10?

How are these verses similar to Christ's words to Peter in Matthew 16:23?

What is the source of the advice you offer to your friends and family members?

5. If you have time, skim through the arguments of Job's friends, Job's defense, and God's confrontation of Job in chapters 3–41. What does Job learn from his sufferings?

6. What happened to Job at the end of the book (Job 42:10–17)?

Is the mother of his new family the same woman as the wife mentioned in chapter 2? Why, or why not, do you think?

7. Did Job's wife benefit in any way from her experiences?

In what ways did she help or hinder her husband in his sufferings?

What do you learn about God from the example of her life? How can you be sure to give godly advice that others will follow?

*T*he Book of Job is a literary masterpiece of suffering and searching, as well as a philosophical penetration into the nature of God and his dealings with humanity. It has much to teach us that would merit a deeper study than we can attempt in this chapter. Our purpose is to focus on the character of Job's wife, and to apply the warning of her example to our own lives.

There are two important questions to consider. First, why was Job's wife spared, when all the rest of Job's family, crops, servants, flocks, and physical health were destroyed by Satan? Second, although Job's wife was not physically cast out, she was sternly rebuked for the poor advice she offered her husband; therefore, what wrong attitudes were revealed in her single comment that made Job react strongly and that resulted in her being left out of the rest of the narrative? Although she did not die and was not divorced, she does not appear in the story again. Even though we infer that she is the same wife who provided Job with ten children at the end of the book, she is not mentioned as a full partner in his blessing from God.

As we look for answers to these challenging questions we must be mindful of the fact that only two verses concern Job's wife in the entire book; and we must be on our guard against irresponsible interpretation or distortion of the context. Whatever we suppose must have happened should always be laid before God, so that we remain open to receive whatever he would teach us through this woman.

Spared by Satan

Satan's challenge to God was that he could compel Job to curse God to his face if only Satan were given permission to touch (i.e., destroy) Job's assets—his personal family, wealth, and health. God showed his confidence in Job through his willingness to allow such a test. The single restriction on the test was that Job's life might not be taken.

Immediately Job received back-to-back messages that all of his flocks, crops, servants, and children had been destroyed (Job 1:13–19). His response to this devastating news is amazing.

> At this, Job got up and tore his robe and shaved his head. Then he fell to the ground in worship and said: "Naked I came from my mother's womb, and naked I will depart. The LORD gave and the LORD has taken away; may the name of the LORD be praised." In all this, Job did not sin by charging God with wrongdoing (Job 1:20–22).

In order to win his wager, Satan clearly needed to try another strategy, and for this purpose he had craftily preserved an "ace-in-the-hole"—Job's wife. Nothing in his bargain with God would have prevented him from killing her along with Job's ten children; only because of the possibility of his accomplishing more evil by using her to influence her husband to curse God did Satan spare her life. Since the initial, external assault on Job had failed to achieve the desired effect, Satan turned his efforts in a new direction: destroying Job's integrity.

We don't see Satan appearing in physical form to tempt Job's wife as he did with Eve. But consider how well she served his purposes. Her statement "Curse God and die!" (Job 2:9) is the only instance recorded in the book in which Satan's objective was explicitly articulated to Job. If instead of simply scanning the list of his afflictions we can appreciate the depth of his agony, we will have some idea of the strength of the temptation to follow his wife's advice. Had Job yielded at that point Satan would have been the victor, and the whole book, indeed the whole world, would have proceeded very differently. We can thank God for protecting us from such horrible speculations.

But the fact that Satan could even attempt to ruin a man's relationship with God by exploiting his relationship of trust with his wife is a strong challenge to me to share only God's wisdom with my family and friends, and to beware of false influences. If Satan spared Job's wife because he thought he could work greater harm through her than without her, I must be watchful for what evil he may be trying to accomplish through me. Watchful, but not fearful, however, since I can be confident that Christ has already won the final victory over sin and death (Heb. 2:14–15).

Spurned by Spouse

Apart from serving Satan's purpose in his wager with God, what was there about his wife's advice that caused such a strong rejection from Job? In a word, blasphemy.

God had clearly set forth the punishment for such a crime against his name.

> If anyone curses his God, he will be held responsible: anyone who blasphemes the name of the LORD must be put to death. The entire assembly must stone him. Whether an alien or native-born, when he blasphemes the Name, he must be put to death (Lev. 24:15–16).

Many other verses in the Bible elaborate on God's severe view of blasphemy, including Exodus 20:1–7 (part of the Ten Commandments) and Matthew 12:30–32, where Jesus said:

> "He who is not with me is against me, and he who does not gather with me scatters. And so I tell you, every sin and blasphemy will be forgiven men, but the blasphemy against the Spirit will not be forgiven. Anyone who speaks a word against the Son of Man will be forgiven, but anyone who speaks against the Holy Spirit will not be forgiven, either in this age or in the age to come."

There can be no mercy for one who curses the name of our maker and model for holiness. Yet this is what Job's wife precisely and deliberately suggested that he do—"Curse God and die!" Fortunately, Job rejected her advice with all the strength of his being. "'You are talking like a foolish woman. Shall we accept good from God, and not trouble?' In all this, Job did not sin in what he said" (Job 2:10).

Stuck in Suffering

How could a wife respond to her husband's suffering in such an unsympathetic way? Her comment was actually a reflection of her own despair. Since Job must have shared all of his children, servants, and flocks with his wife, she, too, had lost everything. Yet, we do not see her progressing out of her profound grief and confusion to a place of acceptance and worship, as Job did throughout the course of the book. Her outburst in favor of blasphemy suggests that she turned instead in the direction of hopeless bitterness. She saw no possibility of discovering any explanations for her troubles, and she had no faith to believe that God *was* in control, even though his purposes and plans were beyond her comprehension. Without any way to deal with their mutual suffering, she was unable to cope with the additional agony of Job's painful sores (Job 2:7). One more undeserved disaster, one more unanswered question were more than she could bear. Unwilling to expose her wounds before the Lord in order to receive his comfort, she could never comprehend, not to mention share, Job's attitude of long-suffering and faith. From such a state it is but a small step downward to the conclusion that nothing has meaning, and then just another step to open disobedience or defiance of God (with the argument "If nothing matters, what is the point of obedience?"). To Job's wife, an early death, even by stoning or the striking of God's hand against her husband, seemed preferable to his unrelenting agony.

Be honest. Have you ever felt this way? Disease, disaster, and despair threaten to swallow you up, until death itself seems to offer the only way of escape. Listen to God. For the hurt there is hope, for the fear faith. He does not promise a walk down Easy Street the moment you put your hand in his. It may be down Hard Road instead, but he is always with you. Though your grasp may falter at times, his hold on you is everlasting.

> Yea, though I walk through the valley of the shadow of death, I will fear no evil: for thou art with me; thy rod and thy staff they comfort me. Thou preparest a table before me in the presence of mine enemies: thou anointest my head with oil; my cup runneth over. Surely goodness and mercy

shall follow me all the days of my life: and I will dwell in
the house of the LORD for ever (Ps. 23:4–6, KJV).

Shortsighted Suggestion

In addition to being stuck in her own suffering, Job's
wife seemed determined to impress on Job the hopeless-
ness of his situation. Without being able to see out of her
own hole, she discouraged him from looking beyond his
misery. Entrenched in her own grief, she offered no sympathy, no comfort, no sensitivity whatsoever to her husband's needs. She had to be sure that Job was well aware
of her negative outlook, but she was not open to being
comforted or guided by her husband's larger view or by
God's perfect perspective.

Often I find myself acting too much like a mother hen
clucking over her chicks. I offer profound insights into
other peoples' lives free for the taking (and they are worth
the fee!). Always on the alert to insure that my children,
husband, and friends behave and learn appropriately from
every situation, I may miss an important lesson for my own
life. Job's wife thought she knew what Job ought to do, but
she was quite blind to her own need. She reminds me that
my first responsibility is to be more open to what the Lord
would teach *me*, and more relaxed in allowing him to guide
his other children directly and according to his own perfect will for them.

Job's wife had blocked herself off from the Lord's comfort and was trying to interfere in his relationship with Job
as well. For his part, Job was in a state of shock, confusion,
and pain: yet, he was willing to let God enlighten him
through his experiences (see Prov. 2:1–8). He answered his
wife appropriately. "You are talking like a foolish woman.
Shall we accept good from God, and not trouble?" (Job
2:10). A footnote in the New International Version points

out that his word *foolish* actually denotes *moral deficiency*, an apt description of her character.

If Satan spared Job's wife because of his mischief, God spared her because of his mercy. As far as her advice and her personality are concerned, she became of no account at that very point in the narrative. She is referred to later, however (in Job 19:17 and 31:10), and she must have survived to bear Job's subsequent children of blessing (Job 42:12–13). Still, her wrong attitude caused her to lose all opportunity for development, both as an individual and as a character in the book.

Job's friends were more persistent with their false accusations and poor advice than was Job's wife. They were sternly rebuked by God for their wrong judgments. "I am angry with you . . . because you have not spoken of me what is right, as my servant Job has" (Job 42:7). They were wrong, but they became reconciled at the end when God accepted Job's sacrifice and intercessory prayer in their behalf and allowed them to celebrate his double portion of prosperity. From their story we should learn not that it is wrong to question God but that it is wrong to refuse to heed his answers.

To speak the truth about God requires diligent study and prayer. It is not easy to keep from embroidering his Word with our own thoughts and desires or from wallowing in our own experiences. But the tremendous challenge of Job's wife is that if we fail to fulfill the important responsibility of leading others to praise rather than to curse God's name, Satan is only too happy to add more aces to his deck of destruction. On the other hand, God desires

> to comfort all who mourn,
>   and provide for those who grieve in Zion—
> to bestow on them a crown of beauty instead of ashes,
>   the oil of gladness instead of mourning,
>   and a garment of praise instead of a spirit of despair.

They will be called oaks of righteousness, a planting
   of the LORD for the display of his splendor (Isa. 61:2–3).

Will you allow him to do this in your life, so that you do
not find yourself set aside in the same way as Job's wife,
and for the same reason?

4

Leah

Primary Scripture Reading	Supplementary Reference
Genesis 29–44	Philippians 4

Questions for Study and Discussion

1. Skim Genesis 29 and 30, noting verses that give details about the appearance and character of the sister-wives Rachel and Leah. Which character do you think you most closely resemble?

   Which woman provides the more godly example?

2. Describe their father Laban, using these chapters and anything else you remember about him. Why did he deceive Jacob in this way?

3. How did Leah initially feel about her father's trick and Jacob's reaction?

   Did anything happen in the course of time to change her predicament?

Could she have done anything to improve her situation?

4. What was the constant desire of Leah's heart?

   Do you think she ever achieved her goal? Did the effects of Jacob's favoritism diminish after Rachel's death?

5. What does the scene concerning the mandrakes signify to you (Gen. 30:14–16)?

   What insights into the personalities of the two women and the social dynamics of Jacob's household do you get from this passage?

6. If your Bible translation has footnotes or marginal references, trace the meanings of the names Leah gave to her children and those of her handmaid. What evidence of Leah's manner of coping with her feelings of rejection do you find?

   How did God comfort her?

   Through which of her offspring did God choose to send the Messiah (Gen. 49:10–12; Mic. 3:2; Rev. 5:5)? How would that fact have been an extra blessing to Leah had she known it?

7. Have you, like Leah, been rejected in some way? How could you apply her example, and experience God's comfort, in the midst of your difficult circumstances?

*G*enesis 29 tells how Jacob met and fell in love with his cousin and endured seven years of hard labor to win her as his bride. His deep love and devotion to Rachel have inspired marriage dreams and promises ever since that day. Then there was Leah. Her story can also inspire us by showing us the way to turn over to God our feelings of hurt and rejection.

We have seen in our study so far that Hagar, Zipporah, and Job's wife had to be sent away, sent back, or totally ignored because their personalities or advice were incompatible with God's purposes. They could not ultimately contradict his plans, but neither did they cooperate fully with them. Leah's situation was different. She was willing to obey her father, her husband, and her God, but she experienced rejection anyway, in that her husband Jacob always preferred her sister. This prejudice was undeserved, but no less painful. The way Leah learned to deal with her unhappiness through many years can encourage each one of us whenever we feel unjustly unappreciated.

Face Facts

Laban, Rebekah's brother and the father of Rachel and Leah, is a complex character worthy of study in his own right. For our purposes, however, it is sufficient to note from the passages in which he is mentioned (Gen. 24–31, passim) that he was wealthy, powerful, and used to getting his own way, which was usually devious. Consider the record of Jacob's initial interviews with his father-in-law.

> As soon as Laban heard the news about Jacob, his sister's son, he hurried to meet him. He embraced him and kissed him and brought him to his home, and there Jacob told him all these things. Then Laban said to him, "You are my own flesh and blood." After Jacob had stayed with him for a whole month, Laban said to him, "Just because you are a relative of mine, should you work for me for nothing? Tell me what your wages should be." Now Laban had two daughters; the name of the older was Leah, and the name of the younger was Rachel. Leah had weak eyes, but Rachel was lovely in form, and beautiful. Jacob was in love with Rachel and said, "I'll work for you seven years in return for your younger daughter Rachel." Laban said, "It is better to give her to you than some other man. Stay here with me." So Jacob served seven years to get Rachel, but they seemed like only a few days to him because of his love for her. Then Jacob said to Laban, "Give me my wife. My time is completed, and I want to lie with her." So Laban brought together all the people of the place and gave a feast. But when evening came, he took his daughter Leah and gave her to Jacob, and Jacob lay with her. And Laban gave his servant girl Zilpah to his daughter as her maidservant. When morning came, there was Leah! (Gen. 29:13–25).

What a crafty man! It was typically Laban's style to make agreements with Jacob and later to change their meaning to suit his own interests. Here we see him cheating Jacob of his desired bride after extracting seven years' labor from his love-struck nephew. He passed Leah off to Jacob in the manner of a dishonest businessman getting rid of damaged merchandise at full price, which was exactly his attitude no matter what noble motives he might have claimed about the social awkwardness of a younger daughter marrying before the elder one (Gen. 29:26). It really was of no concern to him how Jacob or Leah or Rachel might have felt about his deceitful tactics, nor what consequences might ensue for the entire family. And there were plenty.

At first we are not told exactly how Leah felt about being dumped on Jacob in this way. She may even have been secretly pleased and hopeful that Jacob would accept her. But Jacob made no effort to hide his sense of outrage: "What is this you have done to me? I served you for Rachel, didn't I? Why have you deceived me?" (Gen. 29:15). How could Leah have failed to realize Jacob's bitter disappointment, or to feel deeply hurt by it? Although Jacob honorably fulfilled his obligation to Leah by finishing out the bridal week with her (Laban had skillfully trapped him, and he had no real choice in the matter), it was obvious that he couldn't wait to gain the real desire of his heart. Finally, the week was over. "Jacob lay with Rachel also, and he loved Rachel more than Leah" (Gen. 29:30). Again, the fact was obvious to all, and most cruelly felt by Leah.

Sometimes it is hard for us to face facts. We try to see only what we want to see, instead of what is really there but unpleasant. The Talmud puts it thus: "We see things as we are, not as they are." We act as though our pretending a problem does not exist will make it go away, like the ostrich with his head buried in the sand. Or we devote ourselves to unraveling a marginal snag in our affairs rather than attacking the core of the difficulty. Much as she might have wished it otherwise, there was no physical remedy for Leah's weak eyes, and Jacob's preferential love for Rachel could not be altered. Leah had to learn to accept the facts of her situation before she could begin to live with them or grow by means of them. How have you faced the facts of your life?

Confess Feelings

To accept the way things are and to admit that we might prefer them to be otherwise are two different matters. Our first clue to the way Leah handled her hurt feelings comes in Genesis 29:31: "When the LORD saw that Leah was not loved, he opened her womb, but Rachel was barren." Of course, we know that "nothing in all creation is hidden from God's sight. Everything is uncovered and laid bare before the eyes of him to whom we must give account" (Heb. 4:13).

God didn't need Leah to inform him of the facts, any more than he must depend on us for his omniscience today. We don't see Leah pouring out her feelings to the Lord in tearful vows either, as Hannah did in 1 Samuel 1. But we get the impression that Leah's relationship with God was steady and sustaining, so that he was tenderly aware of her situation and able to meet her needs with his sufficiency at every moment of tension. Leah's personality did not incline her to stir up hostility within the household; but she never could have withstood the pressures of her husband's disfavor and her sister's jealousy without knowing the constant comfort of communion with her God. Because she honestly expressed her desires before the Lord he was pleased to see, to listen, and to answer (Gen. 29:31–32; 30:17).

If we are examining Leah for her honest expression of feelings, we must explore the full range of her behavior. The passage concerning the mandrakes does not portray either of Jacob's wives in a very favorable light.

> During wheat harvest, Reuben went out into the fields and found some mandrake plants, which he brought to his mother Leah. Rachel said to Leah, "Please give me some of your son's mandrakes." But she said to her, "Wasn't it enough that you took away my husband? Will you take my son's mandrakes too?" "Very well," Rachel said, "he can

sleep with you tonight in return for you son's mandrakes."
So when Jacob came in from the fields that evening, Leah
went out to meet him. "You must sleep with me," she said.
"I have hired you with my son's mandrakes." So he slept
with her that night (Gen. 38:14–16).

These verses give us a glimpse into what may have been
years of bitter rivalry between the sister-wives. The tension
would truly have become intolerable had not Leah taken
refuge in God's love and blessing. Once again, "God listened to Leah, and she became pregnant and bore Jacob a
fifth son" (Gen. 30:17). Rachel had to wait.

Focus on God

The course of Leah's steadfast devotion to God, the secret
of her survival, is best seen in those verses in which she
gives names to her sons and the sons of her handmaid.
Each of the names reflects the honest yearnings of her
heart, but always with renewed hope and never in anger
or bitterness. A chart will help us to see the sequence and
significance of these names, as Leah continually chose to
concentrate on her positive feelings and her trust in God.

Name	Translation	Verse
Reuben (Gen. 29:32)	See a Son—sounds like Hebrew for, He has seen my misery.	"It is because the LORD has seen my misery. Surely my husband will love me now."
Simeon (Gen. 29:33)	One who hears	"Because the LORD has heard that I am not loved, he gave me this one too."
Levi (Gen. 29:34)	Attached	"Now at last my husband will become attached to me, because I have borne him three sons."
Judah (Gen. 29:35)	Praise	"This time I will praise the LORD."

Issachar (Gen. 30:18)	Reward	"God has rewarded me for giving my maid-servant to my husband."
Zebulun (Gen. 30:28)	Honor, or Dwelling Place	"God has presented me with a precious gift. This time my husband will treat me with honor, because I have borne him six sons."

In contrast to these hope-filled meanings, the names that Rachel chose for the children of her maidservant and later for her own children reflect her spirit of discontent.

Name	Translation	Verse
Dan (Gen. 30:6)	He has Vindicated	"God has vindicated me; he has listened to my plea and given me a son."
Naphtali (Gen. 30:8)	My Struggle	"I have had a great struggle with my sister, and I have won."
Joseph (Gen. 30:24)	May He Add	"May the LORD add to me another son."
Ben-Oni (Gen. 35:18)	Son of My Trouble	
Renamed Benjamin by Jacob (Gen. 35:18)	Son of My Right Hand	

When Leah countered Rachel's tactics by offering her servant Zilpah to Jacob, she still chose joyful names to express her hopes for the future rather than names that expressed her disappointments concerning the past.

Name	Translation	Verse
Gad (Gen. 30:11)	Good Fortune	"What good fortune!"
Asher (Gen. 30:13)	Happy	"How happy I am! The women will call me happy."

Fatal Favoritism

It would be nice to imagine that after the death of his beloved Rachel, Jacob came to have more appreciation of Leah's faithfulness. Unfortunately, there is no Bible verse that suggests such a happy ending to her story. Instead we find that just as Jacob preferred Rachel so he openly favored her two offspring, Joseph (Gen. 37:3) and Benjamin (Gen. 42:38 and 44:18–33), a bias that only served to exacerbate the jealous rivalry that already seethed within their home. In fact, the tragic consequences of playing favorites among one's children or wives are evident from the beginning to the end of Jacob's life.

This pattern leads us to consider two questions: How does Jacob's example challenge us to be more fair, if not equal, in our love and care for our children; and how can we find fulfillment if we live in homes where we do not receive the love we need and deserve, while someone or something else receives preferential treatment?

There is a folk rhyme that states,

> For every trouble under the sun,
>   There is an answer or there is none.
> If there be one, try to find it.
>   If there be none, never mind it.

Leah's situation in life did not drastically improve. In spite of her devotion to God she never gained the favor in her husband's eyes that Rachel enjoyed. Yet she seemed to achieve a contentment through her relationship with the Lord that her sister never attained. When we feel disappointed, hurt, or rejected because of a situation that we cannot change, we must learn what it is to persevere as Leah did. If we will face the facts, confess our feelings, and focus on God for strength and encouragement, we, too, can experience his precious comfort, even in the midst of unrelenting trials.

> Rejoice in the Lord always. I will say it again: Rejoice! Let your gentleness be evident to all. The Lord is near. Do not be anxious about anything, but in everything, by prayer and petition, with thanksgiving, present your requests to God. And the peace of God, which transcends all understanding, will guard your hearts and your minds in Christ Jesus (Phil. 4:4–7).

5

Lot's Wife

Primary Scripture Reading	Supplementary References
Genesis 11–19	Deuteronomy 17
	1 Kings 10–11
	Isaiah 1:9
	Matthew 5:13; 10:15
	Luke 12, 17
	John 3, 14
	Romans 9
	1 Corinthians 3:15
	2 Corinthians 12
	Revelation 11:8

Questions for Study and Discussion

1. Why did God destroy Sodom and Gomorrah? Was he acting in anger or in mercy? (Consider Gen. 14, 18, and 19.)

2. Is God "Judge of all the earth" (Gen. 18:25)?

   How does he judge your life? What excuses do you offer for your sins? How will you escape destruction?

3. What commands did the angels give to Lot? What reasons did God have for these commands?

   How obedient was Lot? How was his entire family affected by his actions?

4. Where, do you think, did Lot find his wife in the first place?

   What criteria would he have used in choosing a woman to marry?

5. Where is your treasure, and thus your heart?

   How trapped are you by your appetites, accumulated possessions, personal affections?

   If your city were about to blow up, what or whom would you try to save?

6. Why did Jesus say, "Remember Lot's wife" (Luke 17:32)? What applications was he making, based on her story? How does his reference affect the historicity of Genesis 19?

7. Examining your response to God, might you be a pillar of salt, or the "salt of the earth" (Matt. 5:13)?

Do you look backward to the things you had or were, or are you focusing on God's blessings to come? How can you turn yourself in the right direction?

*J*esus said, "Remember Lot's wife." Yet, we are never told her name, she has no speaking part in the Bible, and she is mentioned in only a few verses. How can we remember a woman about whom we know so little, and why is she so important?

We can find additional clues to this woman's personality by examining the character of her family and city, and we can learn several significant principles from her disobedience and her destruction. Her husband Lot, who was Abraham's nephew, was an individual who thought primarily of his own needs and desires. When Abraham offered him first choice of all the land he could see, Lot immediately chose the greenest pastures for himself. In Genesis 19, he appeared to value his angelic visitors more highly than his own family, opting to offer his daughters to the rioting Sodomites rather than to violate his code of hospitality. Lot's failures cannot be denied, even in regard to his own selfish goals. Having picked the best land, Lot had to be rescued and restored to it by Abraham in a counterattack against the pagan kings. Later Lot's guests had to reach out to retrieve him and strike the rioters with blindness in order to protect him and his household. Lot's best efforts to convince his future sons-in-law to leave Sodom were rejected as being weak humor. The last scene in which we see Lot is filled with drunkenness and incest. Surely he is one of the most pitiable characters in the Bible.

What about Sodom? Genesis 19:5 makes it obvious that homosexuality was practiced openly there, and we have evidence of other sexual sins as well. Passages in Isaiah (1:9), Matthew (10:15), Romans (9:29), and Revelation (11:8) indicate the proverbial depravity of the place, which is supported by other historical writings and archaeological findings. When the Lord made a special visit to determine whether the outcry against Sodom was warranted, he could not find even ten righteous people for whom to save it. Still, Lot chose to live there and immerse himself and his family in that ungodly environment. He even rose to a position of leadership, perhaps through his marriage. Rather than being shocked at God's destruction of Sodom, we ought really to marvel at his mercy in delivering Lot and his daughters out of the city.

God sent two angels to warn Lot about the impending disaster and to command him to leave the city.

> With the coming of dawn, the angels urged Lot, saying, "Hurry! Take your wife and your two daughters who are here, or you will be swept away when the city is punished." When he hesitated, the men grasped his hand and the hands of his wife and of his two daughters and led them safely out of the city, for the LORD was merciful to them. As soon as they had brought them out, one of them said, "Flee for your lives! Don't look back, and don't stop anywhere in the plain! Flee to the mountains or you will be swept away!" (Gen. 19:15–17).

There were three commands: (1) Hurry. (2) Get far from the area, all the way to the mountains. (3) Don't look back. Lot failed on all three counts. Instead of responding with grateful and hasty obedience, the family seemed indecisive about leaving Sodom, and even when they did, Lot whined until the Lord agreed to let them flee only as far as Zoar, a little town in the plain. And Lot's wife did look back and was turned to a pillar of salt. There is nothing more than half-hearted compliance in these behaviors, a far cry from the deep faith response attained by Lot's Aunt Sarah and Uncle Abraham.

In spite of her depraved environment and her lack of spiritual leadership from her husband, it is important to notice that Lot's wife was still held strictly accountable for her individual act of disobedience. Have you ever defended your actions with excuses like, "It's not my fault. I was brought up this way"; or "My husband should have done thus and so, then I wouldn't be in this mess"? Whenever we are tempted to blame other people or circumstances for our troubles, we should remember Lot's wife.

Why did she look back? Clearly, she disobeyed God's expressed command, but her attitude does not seem to be one of defiance. It was not "I can if I want to," so much as "I just can't help myself." She was simply unable to resist one last look at her hometown. We can easily imagine both good and bad excuses for her backward glance:

1. She was lovingly *concerned* for the remainder of her family left behind in Sodom.
2. She was simply *curious* to see the destruction God had promised.
3. Her heart was too *caught up* in her possessions and lifestyle left behind.
4. She was afraid of the future, and was trying to *cling* to the familiar past as long as she could.

Concerned, curious, caught up, or clinging—whatever her reasons, nothing could justify her disobedience. The fact remains that she disobeyed God's specific orders and reaped an instantaneous, irreversible consequence. Each of us should learn that our actions cannot be rationalized or retracted without paying a permanent price.

In 1 Samuel 16:7 we read, "The LORD seeth not as man seeth; for man looketh on the outward appearance, but the LORD looketh on the heart" (KJV). The same thought is expressed more strongly in Hebrews 4:12–13:

> The word of God is living and active. Sharper than any double-edged sword, it penetrates even to dividing soul and spirit, joints and marrow; it judges the thoughts and attitudes of the heart. Nothing in all creation is hidden from God's sight. Everything is uncovered and laid bare before the eyes of him to whom we must give account.

God's penetrating judgment at once spares us and condemns us, since our hearts are indeed laid bare before him. There is *no* excuse for sin. Christ used the example of Lot's wife in the context of a solemn warning of impending judgment (Luke 17:28–33). When that day of judgment comes, will you be saved, "but only as one escaping through the flames" (1 Cor. 3:15)? Remember Lot's wife.

God is not capricious. He does not delight in setting traps for his people so that he can invent clever punishments for them, saying, "One glance and I'll zap you into a pillar of salt!" Eve is one example that we are wrong to conceive of God's rules as an arbitrary exercise of his power. For our benefit he invites each of us to participate in the blessings that follow from obedience. God has reasons for his rules. In his Word he provides directions as to the right and wrong paths for us and tells us the destinations we can expect to reach on each.

Did Lot's wife feel that she didn't need to take God literally, or that it wouldn't matter if she took just one little peek over her shoulder? Perhaps you think that God should be more lovingly lenient over such seemingly trivial details, and that he is entitled to crack down on us only for big sins. But the whole Bible shows us that our behavior in small things reflects the attitudes of our hearts, which are God's ultimate concern. The kings of Israel were sternly warned against collecting pagan wives and horses, yet Solomon, for all his wisdom, lost his kingdom precisely for committing these offenses (compare Deut. 17:14–17 with 1 Kings 10–11). His excesses culminated in his turning to follow after other gods, to the point of building altars and sacrificing to those gods. It was not simply a matter of horses and wives, after all, but Solomon's attitude for which he was judged (1 Kings 11:11). One thing led to another, as it does with us. From the beginning God established specific behavioral objectives whereby we can measure our growth toward or our drift away from him. Out of love he desires that we obey him so he can bless us, but he will not hesitate to punish those who disregard his Word, just as a wise parent must reinforce the negative rules as part of establishing a positive relationship with his child.

We can trust God to be absolutely fair, both in clear warning and in judgment. We dare not imagine that we can do as we please and then bargain over big and little sins. God is also absolutely holy. Our response to his detailed commands reveals as much about the attitude of our hearts as our outward compliance with broader biblical principles. We fall into the same sin as Lot's wife whenever we yield to temptation and then claim God's compassion, expecting that he could not really have meant we should have obeyed in *that* area, when we are so faithful in general. However, we can rest securely in the knowledge that *all* sins are forgiven under the blood of Christ shed for those who trust in him, but we dare not presume that "good old God" does not care what we do or how we treat his Word. He wants us to love *and* obey him (John 14:15–23). We must be willing to give up our past habits and fears and to move forward in faith whenever he directs us, all the way to the mountains. To look back is to refuse to trust God's plan for what lies ahead. Let us beware of becoming "earthen salt," and strive instead to become "the salt of the earth" which Jesus called his disciples (Matt. 5:13). Remember Lot's wife.

6

Eve

Primary Scripture Reading	Supplementary References
Genesis 1–4	Psalm 119:41–42; 145:3
	Isaiah 55:8–9
	Matthew 4:1–11; 25:10–30
	Ephesians 5:22–23; 6:10–18
	1 Timothy 2
	James 4:7

Questions for Study and Discussion

1. Why did God create Adam?

   Why did he create Eve? What do you think it means to be a help meet (Gen. 2:18, KJV)?

   In your life does the helpmeet concept perhaps apply to situations other than marriage? How can you do better at this assignment?

2. Do you think of yourself as being God's helper?

What kind of help does he need from you (consider Matt. 25 for your answer)?

3. What special purposes and privileges do women enjoy? What do Ephesians 5:22–33 and 1 Timothy 2 say about a woman's place?

   How do you feel about your place in your family, church, job, and community?

4. Why did God command Adam not to eat from the tree of the knowledge of good and evil? Do you think Eve understood this command?

   Why was the tree in the garden in the first place? If God knew Adam and Eve would disobey, why did he allow them to be tempted by the serpent?

5. God cursed Adam "because you listened to your wife." What influence do you have on your family members and close acquaintances through your attitudes, words, and actions?

   How can you develop a more godly influence?

6. Have you ever compelled someone over whom you have
   influence to pay more attention to your words than to
   God's Word? Does that person trust you? Should he or she?

   How can you encourage him or her to follow God's commands when the wisdom of your human counsel is ques-
   tionable?

7. Eve succumbed to the serpent's temptation because she
   changed, added to, and failed to understand God's word.
   Describe a similar experience in which you have yielded to
   temptation.

   How was Christ able to stand firm against Satan's attacks
   (Matt. 4)?

   How can you be more victorious over temptation in the
   future? What specific commands and promises of Scripture
   might you memorize to help you deal with temptation?

*F*ive times in Genesis 1 God saw that his creation
was good. At the end of the chapter "God saw
all that he had made, and it was very good."
Then Genesis 2 gives greater details about Adam and Eve
and their placement in the Garden of Eden. Here, God's
command, his comment, and the couple's response all
include negative words: "you must not eat," "it is not

good," "they felt no shame." Even before the introduction of sin in Genesis 3, we may sense that something is about to go wrong.

What did God have in mind when he created Eve? Did she turn out the way he intended? How could she have avoided falling for the subtle serpent's sinister suggestions? How can we find and follow God's good and perfect will (see Rom. 12:1–2) when we are tempted to disobey? We have much to learn about God, about Satan, and about ourselves as we consider this First Lady of Disobedience, Eve.

Creation of a Helper

When I was about six years old, I enjoyed watching my mother in the kitchen. Everything she did looked easy and fun, and I wanted to help. She let me take over each task while she started on something else. Within a few minutes I would discover that the job I had taken wasn't easy or fun for me, because I lacked my mother's strength and experience. But what she was doing at *that* moment looked really easy and fun! Again, she let me take over. I followed her around the kitchen for an hour, peeling, beating, cracking, or chopping for a minute or two and then giving up.

My mother had to come back and finish everything herself. She might have enjoyed training me, but she also had a responsibility to get dinner on the table. She would say, "I know you want to help, but this is not helping."

Now I say to my own two helpers, "It is only helping if you are really helping." I try to give them jobs that are easy and fun and within their range of success. God wants us to be his helpers in much the same way. We need to learn, as Sarah did, that we are helping him best when we fulfill only the tasks he has assigned to us, no more and no less.

Of course, helping God almost always involves helping others as well. When God first observed, "It is not good for the man to be alone" (Gen. 2:18), he brought all the beasts and birds to Adam "to see what he would name them. But for Adam no suitable helper was found" (Gen. 2:19–20); so he created woman to be man's *help meet* (the word used in KJV). The idea was not merely to provide the man with either a subordinate or a second self, but to create a true companion, one who would be both compatible and compassionate, a full partner in all his joys and sorrows, one with whom he would be able to share himself fully and whom he could fulfill.

More than just an old-fashioned synonym for wife, the words *help meet* describe the supporting role of all Christians. Hebrews 10:24–25 reminds us, "Let us consider how we may spur one another on toward love and good deeds. Let us not give up meeting together, as some are in the habit of doing, but let us encourage one another—and all the more as you see the Day approaching." To be a help-meet in this broader sense is to be of service to all people, whatever our relationship. When we love others in God's name we do not lose our individuality but discover our true identity as his helpers.

Command to Obey

In the sequence of Genesis 2, God told Adam about the forbidden fruit (v. 17) before he created Eve (v. 22). And what did she learn about this crucial command? God's words to Adam were:

> You are free to eat from any tree in the garden; but you must not eat from the tree of the knowledge of good and evil, for when you eat of it you will surely die (Gen. 2:16–17).

But in Genesis 3:2–3, Eve told the serpent:

We may eat fruit from the trees in the garden, but God did
say, "You must not eat fruit from the tree that is in the middle of the garden, and you must not touch it, or you will
die."

What differences are there between these two statements,
and do they matter? Which verses give the more accurate
rendition of God's command?

At first glance, these two passages seem to be saying
about the same thing. But they do not. The differences
become clear when we chart the verses side by side.

Genesis 2:16–17	Genesis 3:2–3
You are free to eat from any tree in the garden	We may eat fruit from the trees in the garden
but you must not eat from the tree	but God did say, "You must not eat fruit from the tree
of the knowledge of good and evil	that is in the middle of the garden
	and you must not touch it
for when you eat of it	or
you will	you will
surely	
die.	die."

God told Adam that the tree embodied the knowledge
of good and evil, but Eve told the serpent only that it was
in the middle of the garden. If she was aware of the power
of the tree, she did not use this information to help herself resist the power of Satan, who was only too glad to sub-
stitute his own cunning version of God's intent:

For God knows that when you eat of it your eyes will be
opened, and you will be like God, knowing good and evil
(Gen. 3:5).

Thus, Eve yielded the security and strength that come only from God's exact words, and Satan moved in. Of course, this does not mean that biblical principles cannot be applied to various circumstances and needs today. But we must be very sure to base our applications on a deep and faithful understanding of God's Word. Accept no substitutes.

Eve's second big mistake was to add to God's command. God had not said that the tree could not be touched. How can we be sure of this? Is it not possible that the phrase was simply left out of Genesis 2:17, and that Eve's quotation was really the more complete? The answer is no, for two reasons. First, when God found Adam and Eve in the garden after their fall into sin, he said to them, "Have you eaten from the tree that I commanded you not to eat from?" (Gen. 3:11). And in cursing Adam he added the explanation, "Because you listened to your wife and ate from the tree about which I commanded you, 'You must not eat of it'" (Gen. 3:17). If God had actually commanded them not to touch the tree, he would have mentioned the fact. Besides, God had placed Adam in the garden "to work it and take care of it" (Gen. 2:15), which must have included permission to touch the trees when necessary.

Second, the whole Bible helps us to know that God is not so arbitrary as Eve makes him appear in her statement. Although his ways are not our ways (Isa. 55:8–9), and his greatness is beyond what we can fathom (Ps. 145:3), we can have confidence that he has perfect, not petty reasons for all he does and says. Eve's adding to his command renders it almost frivolous, and again reveals her lack of deep understanding of God's design.

Perhaps we at times also fail to understand God's design. How can we resist temptation better than Eve did? By asking God for fuller understanding of his purposes, and by simply obeying better, whether or not we are granted such illumination. In the desert Christ became our perfect model when he countered each of Satan's insidious propositions with direct quotations from the Scriptures (Matt. 4:1–11). The result: Satan fled. Though Jesus was aware that he had all the power of the universe at his disposal to claim or renounce his kingdom at any moment, he submitted perfectly to his Father's plan and timing at every step. To resist Satan he used only the resource we, too, have been given— the Word of God. He knew it perfectly, for he *is* the Word. He did not alter or add to it in any way. We, too, must commit ourselves to storing his Word in our hearts daily, so that we may be well-armed against temptation (consider Eph. 6:10–18, Ps. 119, James 4:7). The moment of attack is not the time to begin making weapons; we must study and pray continually. Only then can we hope to face temptation by the power of God's Word with more confidence and strength than Eve displayed.

Corruption

There is another aspect of Eve's disobedience from which we can learn something important. Having succumbed to temptation, how did Eve persuade Adam to eat the fruit with her? Having become corrupt, how did she corrupt her husband also? The key verse is tantalizingly stark: "She also gave some to her husband, who was with her, and he ate it" (Gen. 3:6).

Parenthetically, it may be that this verse raises more questions in our minds than it resolves. Was Adam with her during her encounter with Satan? Why didn't he speak up to protect her or himself? There is certainly no indication that Adam protested or tried to discover the source of the fruit Eve offered him. Was this because he already knew where it came from, since he was there all along, and was only holding back until he was satisfied that nothing terrible seemed to happen when his wife took that first bite?

But let us make two observations about Eve from this verse. Eve did not appear to resort to devious means to persuade Adam to taste the fruit after her. She simply gave it to him and he ate it. Adam trusted his wife perfectly. Of course, with no sin in the world prior to that moment, he would have had no reason not to trust her. Nevertheless, this scene moves me to treasure the high degree of trust my husband has placed in me. We ought not treat lightly the trust people have in us. We should strive to be worthy of it every day, not by merely refraining from bald deception, but by unfailingly encouraging them to do good, and by serving their needs in little as well as big matters.

The second observation about Eve concerns the amount of influence she had over her husband because of their mutual love and trust. He did what she said.

When I step off the curb, my children follow me into the street, trusting that I have indeed checked for traffic. When I give my opinion on whether it would be better at this time to remodel the kitchen than to buy a new car, my husband trusts my advice. These responses from my family are in one sense gratifying, but in another sense they represent a tremendous responsibility. What if I am mistaken in my judgment, in these examples as well as in countless others? Obviously, my children could get hit by a truck, or our budget could be thrown seriously out of balance (not to mention what could happen to our poor old car). I am not the head of the household, yet my family is greatly affected by what I do and say.

And what of my power to destroy a friendship, degrade a minister, dampen a social occasion, or deflate a child's enthusiasm simply by dropping a comment or a sigh into the conversation around the dinner table? I can corrupt those around me just by projecting my own foul mood, for whatever reason. This realization challenges me to gain better control over my thoughts and feelings, as well as my words and deeds, lest I tempt anyone to evil because of our shared relationship of trust.

Consequences

Eve was created to be a suitable helper for Adam. She failed because she did not take God's command seriously enough either to obey it or to depend on it as a strong defense against temptation. She corrupted her husband. What were the consequences? It is not difficult to list quite a few.

1. The possibility of sin entered the world. (Gen. 3:6)
2. Adam, Eve, and Satan were cursed by God. (Gen. 3:14–19)
3. Christ's ultimate victory was foreshadowed. (Gen. 3:15)
4. Pain in childbirth was increased. (Gen. 3:16)
5. Women were placed under their husbands' rule. (Gen. 3:16)
6. Adam and Eve were cast out of Eden, which was sealed against them. (Gen. 3:24)
7. Adam stopped listening to Eve.

But wait! How can I say Adam stopped listening to Eve when I have just finished saying that we women have a great deal of influence over those who trust our words and deeds, and that we ought to be more mindful of that fact? Because I want to make another point here: Adam's big mistake was in obeying his wife *instead of God*. Before the Lord laid his curse on Adam, he said, "Because you listened to your wife and ate from the tree about which I commanded you, 'You must not eat of it'" (Gen. 3:17). Having violated Adam's trust in her, Eve had lost something precious for all time. Adam would have to be more careful from that time forward to check everything for himself. The once-perfect helpmeet was henceforth placed under the rule of her husband, and God made it crystal clear that his Word was the only one that must be adhered to. Is it not also necessary for us to guard against placing those who trust us in the position of having to choose between God's Word and our selfish interests?

It is not easy to speculate on what life in Eden might have been like—a perfect paradise without sin, no sickness or hurt, no fear or doubt. We can only guess as to what could have happened if Eve had resisted Satan, or if Adam had resisted Eve. God is both wise and merciful in not revealing to us too much of that early perfection, since it is so difficult for us sinful beings to comprehend. Yet, there is enough in these first few chapters of the Bible to keep us thinking and growing each time we read them. Obviously, we have not dealt here with every issue concerning Eve that has been raised throughout the centuries. But for me her disobedience represents a challenge to know and stand firmly on the Word of God, and to seek his help against all temptation, for my own good as well as for the sake of my family.

Perhaps you have disobeyed God's Word because you, like Eve, have not known God well enough to take him at his word. Have you diluted the power of the Scriptures to half-strength through your own selections, additions, and transformations, so that you have no defense against temptation when it comes? Then you must choose to take a new direction by drawing comfort and strength from Christ's perfect example of obedience and resistance.

> May your unfailing love come to me, O LORD,
>   your salvation according to your promise;
> then I will answer the one who taunts me,
>   for I trust in your word (Ps. 119:41–42).

Suggestions for Group Leaders

1. Keep in mind that the purpose of group discussion is to help all the members understand the Bible, implement the truths learned, refresh each other by exchanging thoughts, impressions, and ideas, and to support the formation of bonds of friendship.

2. Encourage the members to set aside a daily time for study and prayer.

3. Remind the members to write out answers. Expressing oneself on paper clarifies thoughts and analyzes understanding. Because written answers are succinct and thoughtful, discussion will be enlivened.

4. Be familiar enough with the lesson so you can identify questions that can most easily be omitted if time is short. Select and adapt an appropriate number of questions so that the lesson topic can be completed. Reword the question if the group feels it is unclear. Covering too little material is discouraging to the class. Skip the questions that cover material the class has already discussed. Often the last questions are the most thought-provoking. Choose questions that create lively and profitable interchange of views.

5. Encourage all members to participate. Often the less vocal people have amazingly thoughtful contributions.

6. Keep the group focused on the passage studied, emphasizing that answers should come from Scripture. Steer the discussion away from tangents. Sidestep controversial subjects, Christian causes, political action, and so forth. Ask, "Where did you find that in this passage?" "Did anyone find a thought not yet mentioned?"

7. Pick up on any "live news" of spiritual growth, recent actions taken, honest admissions of inadequacy or failures, and desires for prayer. Be sensitive to "beginners" in the Christian walk, recognizing their need to share new discoveries, joys, commitments, and decisions.

8. Spend time in prayer as you prepare for the lesson. Remember to pray for each member. Pray daily for yourself to have a listening ear, a sensitive heart, and an effervescent and contagious spirit of joy as you lead. Pray you will affirm each member who contributes. Ask God to give you a variety of ways to do this.

Closing Remarks

Prepared closing remarks are valuable (and essential) for clearing up misunderstandings of the passage, further teaching, applying the Scripture to current situations, and for challenging each individual to action. Before the meeting decide on how much time to allow for discussion and closing remarks, and follow the timetable.